# THE
# VIKINGS
## FACT AND FICTION

Adventures of young Vikings in Jorvik

ROBIN PLACE

◆

**Cambridge University Press**

Cambridge
New York New Rochelle
Melbourne Sydney

◆

This book has been produced with the active cooperation of the Jorvik Viking Centre. The publishers would like to thank Richard Hall of the York Archaeological Trust, the site director of the Coppergate dig, and the staff of the centre for their help.

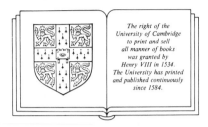

The right of the
University of Cambridge
to print and sell
all manner of books
was granted by
Henry VIII in 1534.
The University has printed
and published continuously
since 1584.

Published by the Press Syndicate of the University of Cambridge
The Pitt Building, Trumpington Street, Cambridge CB2 1RP
32 East 57th Street, New York, NY 10022, USA
10 Stamford Road, Oakleigh, Melbourne 3166, Australia

First published 1985
Reprinted 1987

Printed in Great Britain by Blantyre Printing and Binding

Place, Robin
  The Vikings: fact and fiction: adventures of young Vikings in Jorvik.
  1. Vikings – Social life and customs – Juvenile literature
  I. Title
  948′.02   DL31
  ISBN 0 521 30855 0 hardcover
       0 521 31572 7 paperback

DS

**Illustrations by Chris Ryley**

**Acknowledgements**

Page **4** York Archaeological Trust, M.S. Duffy (top and right), Chris Evans (left); **6** YAT M.S. Duffy (top and bottom), Chris Evans (right) University of York, Environment Archaeology Unit, Andrew Jones (left, inset); **8** YAT Helen Humphreys (left), YAT M.S. Duffy (right), Chris Evans (bottom); **10** YAT M.S. Duffy (top left), YAT (top right), YAT M.S. Duffy (bottom); **12** Chris Evans (left and right), YAT M.S. Duffy (bottom); **14** Universitetets Oldsaksamling, Oslo (top left), YAT M.S. Duffy (top right), The Trustees of the British Museum (bottom left), YAT Sheena Howarth (bottom right); **16** YAT M.S. Duffy (top), YAT Sheena Howarth (left), University of York, Environmental Archaeology Unit, Andrew Jones (right); **18** YAT M.S. Duffy (centre), YAT (bottom); **20** YAT M.S. Duffy (top and bottom), YAT Sheena Howarth (left and right); **22** Chris Evans (top), YAT M.S. Duffy (centre and bottom); **24** YAT Sheena Howarth (top and centre), Chris Evans (left), YAT M.S. Duffy (bottom right); **26** YAT M.S. Duffy (top), Chris Evans (centre right), YAT Sheena Howarth (centre left), YAT M.S. Duffy (centre and bottom); **28** YAT M.S. Duffy (left and right), Chris Evans (bottom); **30** Chris Evans (top), YAT M.S. Duffy (left and right), Chris Evans (bottom); **32** YAT M.S. Duffy (centre).

# What this book is about

These stories are about some of the Viking families who lived long ago in York, which they called 'Jorvik'. We know a great deal about the Vikings although they lived over one thousand years ago. Archaeologists have uncovered the houses where Viking families lived, the hearths on which they cooked and remains of food and clothing which tell us about what they ate and what they wore. Children's toys like bone skates and wooden tops were also found. Many of these discoveries have been made in York in an area called Coppergate, a part of the town of which the name comes from the Viking meaning, 'Cup-makers' street'. Because the ground there has always been wet, all sorts of things were preserved there which normally decay in dry ground. So archaeologists have found out much more about Viking life in York, or 'Jorvik', than has been possible at many other places where the Vikings lived.

Before writing these stories, I went to see all the remarkable finds from the Coppergate dig, and I began to think about what the Jorvik children had to do all day, and what their lives were like through the seasons of the year. They did not go to school, and they could not watch television. They had to amuse themselves, but most of their day must have been filled with jobs to do. They had to help their fathers and mothers, and learn from them the crafts that they would use when they grew up.

These stories are about children who might have lived in Jorvik. But I have not just made these stories up out of my head. I have based them on things that have been found at Jorvik and in other places where the Vikings lived. So that you can judge for yourselves what the evidence is, we have shown these things on the 'How do we know?' fact pages which you will find opposite the story pages.

I hope you will enjoy this journey back in time – by reading the stories, by looking at the evidence here in this book and by going and seeing it for yourself at Jorvik.

*Robin Place*

In this book you will find many pictures of things made of wood. Archaeologists are always very excited to find wooden objects because wood is only preserved in places where the ground is wet (or where the climate is dry and hot, as in Egypt). Luckily the ground under Jorvik has always been wet so that many wooden tools have been found as well as things made of leather and cloth.

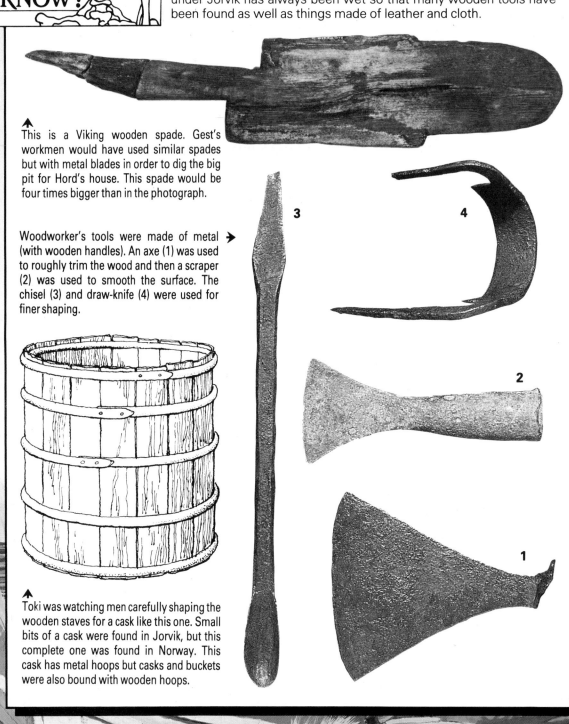

↑ This is a Viking wooden spade. Gest's workmen would have used similar spades but with metal blades in order to dig the big pit for Hord's house. This spade would be four times bigger than in the photograph.

Woodworker's tools were made of metal → (with wooden handles). An axe (1) was used to roughly trim the wood and then a scraper (2) was used to smooth the surface. The chisel (3) and draw-knife (4) were used for finer shaping.

↑ Toki was watching men carefully shaping the wooden staves for a cask like this one. Small bits of a cask were found in Jorvik, but this complete one was found in Norway. This cask has metal hoops but casks and buckets were also bound with wooden hoops.

# Spring: *A New Friend*

Toki was sitting in the sun, watching the men at the wood stall in Jorvik, where he lived. They were making a big wooden cask. He liked the smell of the wood, and the way little shavings curled up as the iron scraper was drawn along each stave.

Toki was stroking a cat. It belonged to Thora, the wife of Snarri the jeweller. The cat's fur was warm; it was the first sunny day of the year. Suddenly the clouds and gloom of winter had gone. Housewives propped open their doors after months of keeping them tightly shut, in spite of the smoke from the fires. Some energetic women were scraping up the smelly rubbish that had been left on the earth floors of their homes all winter. Basketloads of old animal bones and bad vegetables, eggshells and shellfish shells were tipped into the yard behind each house. As the women worked, they shouted to one another, exchanging news.

Toki did not have anyone to play with and he was bored. Suddenly Toki heard his father calling him. As he had nothing special to do, he got up and went home. He saw that something exciting was happening. The remains of the tumbledown house next door were being cleared away. No-one had lived there as long as he could remember. His father was setting men to work, digging old rotten posts out of the ground. Toki was told to help. They were going to build a new house.

Toki wondered who was going to live in the new house. He hoped that there would be a boy for him to play with. There were enough girls in Jorvik already!

Gest, Toki's father, was a clever house-builder. While the workmen were clearing the site, and putting up a new fence round it, he rode into the country with Toki to buy timber for

## HOW DO WE KNOW?

In Jorvik, the walls of wooden houses have been preserved because the ground was wet. In this way, archaeologists have been able to see excactly how houses were constructed. The discovery of these houses was very important because on most Viking excavations archaeologists have only found stains in the ground where the wood has long since rotted away.

◀ This is one of the many wicker-lined cess pits excavated in Jorvik. They were full of slimy black mud. Excavating them is very unpleasant work, but the results are very important. By seiving the mud, botanists have found traces of the food the Vikings ate.

The small inset photograph shows the magnified egg of a whip worm which was also found in a cess pit. This tells us that many of the Jorvik Vikings must have suffered from these worms in their intestines.

Building techniques in Viking times were very simple. No nails or wooden pegs were used. First a rectangular pit was dug and grooved foundation beams were placed around the edges. Wooden upright posts were slotted into the foundation beams and planks were piled up behind the posts to form the outside walls. The photograph below shows the remains of the side wall of a tenth century Jorvik house. ▼

building the house. It would only have one room, and be one storey high. The floor would be dug below ground-level, so that there would not be any draughts. Gest had a friend who was a tree-feller, out in the country. Gest chose the timber he wanted, and arranged that his friend would bring it to Jorvik on his wagon. It would mean several journeys.

It was very exciting when the first wagon-load of timber arrived. Everyone came to watch the unloading, and had advice to offer about how to move the heavy tree-trunks.

Gest had woodworkers with sharp axes ready to hack the tree-trunks into long, flat beams. The wood would be smoothed with knives. While they worked, other men were digging the big pit in which the house was to stand. At last the beams were ready to be lowered into position along each side of the pit. Upright posts were shaped next. They were placed on top of each beam. Wide planks were laid on edge to form the lower part of the house walls. The upright posts kept them jammed against the earth outside. A space was left for the door.

The woodworkers with their axes and knives were very busy hacking and shaping planks for floorboards.

Toki helped to carry the heavy timbers. He felt very important, helping his father with his work. The walls of the house went up and up. At last the rafters of the roof were in place, and wagons full of bundles of reeds came trundling along. They came from the marshes outside Jorvik. The thatcher climbed up his ladder with his tools and set to work. Toki was allowed to carry up the reeds.

Toki had seen the new owner of the house. The man had ridden into Jorvik many times to see how the house was getting on. His name was Hord. He was a small man, with fair hair and a beard and he always looked worried. He took a particular interest in how much space there was between the wall of his house and the house next door.

Behind the house, where a lot of nettles grew, Hord told the workmen where he wanted them to dig the cess pit for the family to use. A man arrived to make the hurdles to make a screen round it. He set upright posts in the ground, and wove split poles in and out. He made more hurdles to lay flat on the ground as a path over the nettles and mud.

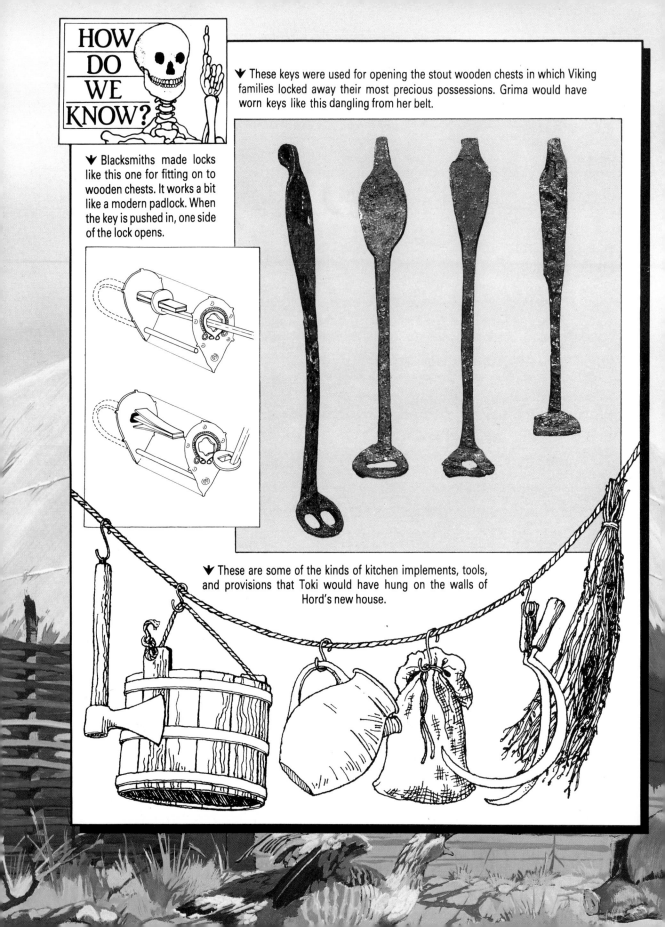

↯ These keys were used for opening the stout wooden chests in which Viking families locked away their most precious possessions. Grima would have worn keys like this dangling from her belt.

↯ Blacksmiths made locks like this one for fitting on to wooden chests. It works a bit like a modern padlock. When the key is pushed in, one side of the lock opens.

↯ These are some of the kinds of kitchen implements, tools, and provisions that Toki would have hung on the walls of Hord's new house.

It was an exciting day when Hord and his family moved into the new house. Toki turned up to help carry things off the wagon (and to have a good look at everything). There were cooking pots packed carefully in baskets of straw; and all sorts of tools that Toki was told to hang on wooden pegs on the walls. Hord and one of his servants carried in a chest of valuables. It was secured by a heavy padlock.

Hord's wife was much younger than he was. She was tall and had long, dark hair. She wore a bunch of keys dangling from her belt, as Toki's mother did. She kept finding fault with everything and everybody. Toki was disappointed to see that the only children were a little girl of about six and a fat little four-year-old boy, who kept crying and running after the woman, hanging on to her long dress. The woman kept hitting the little girl and telling her to get out of the way, but she didn't seem to mind the little boy pulling on her dress all the time.

But to Toki's relief, a cart arrived, driven by a boy of about his own age. This boy had sandy hair and freckles, and a tip-tilted nose. When he saw Toki, he grinned. The tall woman came out of the house and screamed at him to ask why he had been such a long time. The boy seemed used to being shouted at. He got down from the cart wearily, and tried to get a big fat pig to jump out of the back of the cart. Toki went to help. He held the pig's rope and pulled, while the other boy hit it with a stick. Suddenly the pig jumped out of the cart and along the street. Toki was taken by surprise and slipped on some rubbish. He fell over and the pig dragged him along in the dirt until somebody stopped it.

Toki brushed off some of the mud and feathers from the hens that picked and pecked everywhere. He said that his mother was used to it. The other boy said that his name was Bard. The boys walked back together, pulling the pig along, and put it into its new sty. It could not get out through the strong new hurdles. The pig flopped down with a contented grunt.

Toki went home to supper. He was happy. He had found a new friend.

# HOW DO WE KNOW?

These drawings show how Viking wood turners made bowls using a pole lathe. Many different kinds of wood were used but yew, maple or ashwood were the most common types used.

▼ The woodworker first took a piece of wood and roughly shaped it. He then mounted the roughly shaped block on to his pole-lathe.

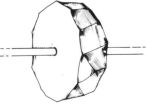

▼ The woodworker then shaped and smoothed the outside first turning the block on the lathe as he worked. Then he cut away the inside with a chisel leaving only a small column of wood in the middle.

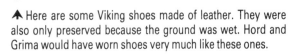

▲ Here are some Viking shoes made of leather. They were also only preserved because the ground was wet. Hord and Grima would have worn shoes very much like these ones.

Many wooden cups and bowls have been found in Jorvik. These have only survived because the ground was wet. Archaeologists know that they were made in Coppergate because the turning cores were found as well as the finished objects. The wooden bowl and turning core you see below were also found in Coppergate. Hord would have made a bowl very much like this one.
▼

▼ Finally, he removed the bowl from the lathe, snapped off the wooden core and smoothed down any remaining bumps.

# Summer: *The Cloak of the Wind*

Toki and Bard became fast friends. They were always to be found together. Toki found out all about Bard's family. His mother had died when his little sister Drifa was born. She was now six. His father had married a new wife, Grima, and she had a little boy Olvir. Bard said sadly that his step-mother did not like him or Drifa very much. Bard and Drifa's clothes were old and ragged, but Olvir always had new clothes and fine leather shoes.

Bard's father Hord worked at a lathe, turning wooden cups and bowls. This machine stood beside his house. This was why he had been so anxious about the space between his house and the next when his house was being built.

Toki liked watching Hord at work, with the block of wood spinning round and round, and taking shape under Hord's skilful hands. But if he asked questions, Hord would tell Toki to go away and not waste his time. Hord had to work fast to make a lot of things to sell. His young wife, Grima, liked to buy expensive food and trinkets for herself, and she bought cloth instead of weaving it at home as most housewives did. She was expecting another baby, and was always complaining that she was too tired to carry out her household tasks. Bard and his little sister had to fetch water from the well and watch food while it was cooking so that it did not burn. Bard liked helping Drifa turn the handle of the cornmill to grind the corn into white flour.

One lovely hot day, Toki and Bard slipped away from their homes and took Drifa down the street to the waterfront to see if any ships were coming in.

They were lucky – a big merchant ship was tying up at the waterfront. The children kept out of the way and a seaman jumped on to the waterfront with a rope. The seamen were

The Vikings were great traders. Many young men went abroad trading to make enough money to buy land to farm. They often had to fight to protect their goods from Viking pirates who lay in wait for ships on the well-known trade-routes. Ships came to Jorvik bringing goods from Scandinavia, Germany and even from the Near East. One silver coin came from Samarkand, and silk came from as far away as China!

People in Jorvik did not buy goods with coins of different values. Goods were bought and sold for a certain weight of gold or silver. Merchants carried a set of folding scales for weighing coins in a round box. Weights and coins were kept in a leather wallet or a linen bag.

⬆ This part of a merchant's scales was excavated in Jorvik. ⬇ Merchants would split coins into small segments if any change was needed.

This piece of rope was preserved in the wet ground of Coppergate. Seamen would have used a lot of rope for tying up their ships at the waterfront in Jorvik.
⬇

tanned with sun and wind, and their clothes were stained with salt. A boy not much older than Bard and Toki was letting out a rope so that the big sail came down in a heap on the deck.

Old Karl, Toki's grandfather, was sitting on the waterfront with his old friend Eymundr. They had bought a barrel of herrings, and were gutting the fish to be dried as food for the winter. Overhead, gulls were wheeling and screaming, looking for titbits. The children stood near the old men and listened to their talk. They watched the crew unload.

The ship had sailed from Iceland to Norway, where the merchants on board had sold some of their cargo of woollen goods and smoked food. They loaded up with Norwegian cooking pots made of soapstone, and other goods. Then they sailed on to Denmark where they had sold things at the market town of Hedeby. There they had taken on Rhenish wine, from Germany, in big pale jars. There they also bought grindstones of a specially hard German rock, so that grit did not get into the flour as it did if the grindstone was made of soft rock. They took on board barrels of herrings. So by the time they reached Jorvik they had a great variety of goods.

One Icelander had a big pile of grey woollen cloaks to sell. He was unloading them, but people who had gathered to see what the ship had brought were laughing at him. It was such a hot day that no-one felt like buying a winter cloak. Winter seemed a long way off.

Suddenly there was a stir among the crowd. A group of men came riding up, and the crowd parted to let them through. They were wearing brightly-coloured clothes. Their cloaks were fastened with shining bronze or silver brooches. They wore silver and gold rings and armlets.

One man in a scarlet tunic had a hawk sitting on his wrist as he rode. His hair was held back by a golden band that shone in the sun. Two hounds sat panting as he reined in his horse. He wore spurs on his heels. He was the king of Jorvik.

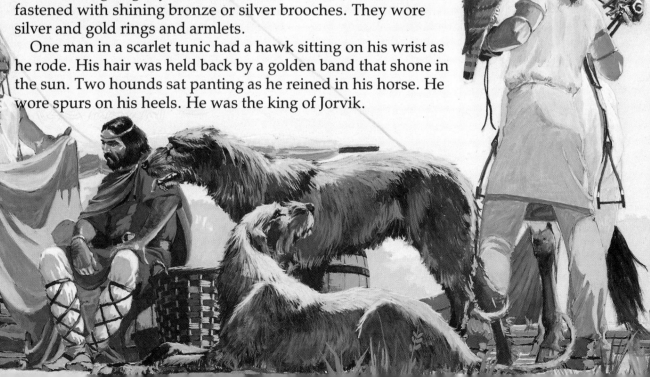

The Vikings liked to decorate the things they made with elaborate patterns. Craftsmen were very artistic, some making brooches and weapons of metal, others carved wood or bone. Look out for the many kinds of decorated objects in this book!

This wooden man's head was carved by a ➤ Viking in Norway. It was part of a decorated wagon. The figurehead on the ship *Karlhofdi* that Karl and Eymundr had sailed on might have looked like this.

▲ Silver brooches like this one were worn by the king and his nobles to fasten their cloaks. Most people wore cheaper brooches made of bronze, copper or lead.

Kings did not pay their attendants regular wages, but rewarded their loyalty and courage with gold arm-rings like this one, or with decorated swords. This arm-ring was found in Ireland.

▲ A spur made of iron. The King would have worn spurs on his heels to make his horse go faster. The king's arrows were ➤ tipped with iron arrow-heads like this one.

The king rode up to the ship. He noticed that the man did not seem to be doing any trading, so he said that he would buy one of his good warm cloaks. He paid the man with silver coins struck in Jorvik. As the king had bought a cloak, people thought they must be good, and everyone started snapping them up. People thrust coins and bits of silver at the Icelander. The children watched fascinated as he scratched each coin to check that it was pure silver, and weighed them on his scales. In hardly any time at all, the cloaks were all gone. The Icelander looked more cheerful, and went off to spend some of his money. The king and his men rode off. They were going hunting in the country outside the town.

The children threw bits of fish guts up to the seagulls and then sat down to listen to what the old men were saying. The coming of the merchant ship had made them remember the fighting ships in which they had gone raiding when they were young.

'The Karlhofdi was the fastest,' Karl recalled, 'The "Man's Head" – and our leader carved the head on the prow himself.'

Eymundr could make up poetry in his head. He never wrote it down, but he could remember long poems. When he was young, he had made up poems about the brave deeds of kings in battles on land and sea. On his travels he had recited them before the kings, who had rewarded him with smart clothing, gold arm-rings and good swords.

Sometimes Eymundr would eat with Toki's family, and after supper he would recite some of his poems when they were sitting round the fire. In the poems about sea-battles (which Toki liked best) Eymundr never said 'ship', but used expressions that made people see the ship speeding over the waves: 'the horse of the gull's track', or 'the raven of the wind'. Everyone knew what he meant as they had often heard the expressions.

'There's no better sight,' said Karl, taking the last fish out of the barrel, 'than a longship with her sail hauled up, and the wind filling it.'

'Ah yes,' mused Eymundr, 'the sail, the cloak of the wind.' He got up to go home.

And always after that, when Toki and his friends saw anyone wearing a grey Icelandic cloak they used to think of the sail of a speeding longship, 'the cloak of the wind'.

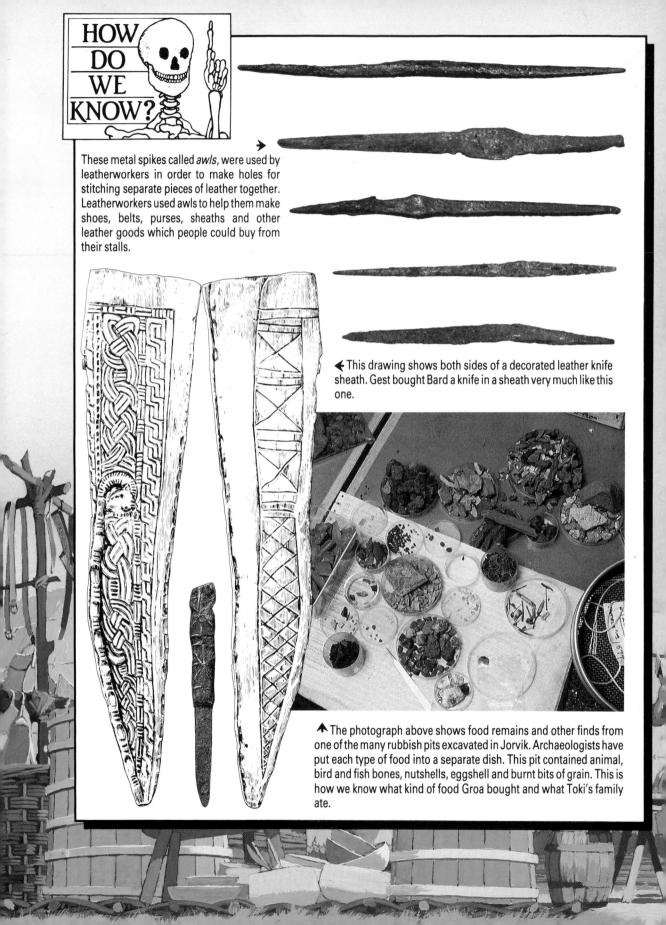

## HOW DO WE KNOW?

These metal spikes called *awls*, were used by leatherworkers in order to make holes for stitching separate pieces of leather together. Leatherworkers used awls to help them make shoes, belts, purses, sheaths and other leather goods which people could buy from their stalls.

◄ This drawing shows both sides of a decorated leather knife sheath. Gest bought Bard a knife in a sheath very much like this one.

▲ The photograph above shows food remains and other finds from one of the many rubbish pits excavated in Jorvik. Archaeologists have put each type of food into a separate dish. This pit contained animal, bird and fish bones, nutshells, eggshell and burnt bits of grain. This is how we know what kind of food Groa bought and what Toki's family ate.

# Autumn: *Fire!*

There was frost in the air in the mornings, and colourful toadstools sprang up in odd corners of the yards. All over Jorvik people were killing their pigs and were smoking the meat to eat through the winter. There were terrible screeches and snorts as the pigs tried to escape when they were let out of the sties to be killed. Bard and Toki watched. It was very exciting. The street was slippery with cowpats as cattle from the countryside were driven into the town also to be killed. The hides would be tanned for leather, and made into shoes, belts, and sheaths for knives, to be sold on the leatherworkers' stalls. Many animals were killed in the autumn as it was hard to feed beasts through the winter.

Bard's step-mother died that autumn. She gave birth to a baby boy, but she caught some infection and both she and the baby died. Hord was very sad, but Bard and his sister Drifa had a happier time as Toki's mother looked after the family. Every evening they all crowded into Toki's house to eat together. One of the first things that Groa, Toki's mother, did was to tell Hord to buy shoes for Bard and Drifa. She herself wove some cloth and made them new clothes. Gest, Toki's father, bought Bard a leather belt and a little knife in a sheath to hang on it. Hord was so grateful for their kindness that he made the family a set of lovely smooth wooden bowls.

Groa took Drifa shopping to teach her to be a good housewife when she grew up and got married. The boys went too. They liked looking at all the food displayed for sale. There were hares from the country, pigeons, chickens, joints of meat, and all sorts of fish and shellfish. When Groa picked up something to see how big it was, clouds of flies flew off it with a great buzz.

This is an alphabet of letters called runes. These letters are made up of straight lines because they were meant to be carved on sticks of wood and it is easier to cut straight lines than curves on wood. The alphabet shown here is one that was used after the time that Thorfast lived in Jorvik, but you will find all the letters you need for writing your name and secret messages.

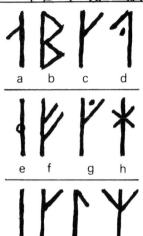

a b c d

e f g h

i k l m

n o p q

r s t u v w

x y z

The Vikings used to write their names on things they used, and on gravestones. Travellers sometimes set up a rune stone to show that they had visited a distant place. Runes on a rock in the far north of Greenland tell us that three Vikings camped there all one winter. Runes were invented long before the Viking Age, and the letters changed as time went by. There were only sixteen letters in the alphabet the Vikings used. This

f u t h a r k

was called the 'futhark' after the first six letters. This sixteen letter alphabet is the one Thorfast would have used for carving Toki and Bard's names on their combs.

▲ A Viking comb and comb case. Many combs were found in Jorvik. They were made from the antlers of red deer. The drawing on the left shows how the comb-maker cut pieces from the antlers to make combs. The drawing on the right shows all of the different stages of making a comb. Thorfast would probably have made combs very much like the one above.

Once he had cut out the pieces of antler for making the comb he would then smooth them down and fix all of the individual parts together by using small metal nails. The comb-maker would then decorate the comb's plates with various geometric patterns, after which he cut the comb's teeth using a fine saw.

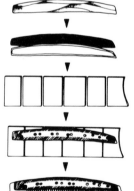

Groa bought new stools from the wood stall for Bard's family to sit on, and a spade so that Toki and Bard could dig a new rubbish pit in the yard. There was now a lot more rubbish – animal bones, shellfish shells, fur from hares and feathers from pigeons, chickens and geese – as Groa was cooking for two families.

Grima's spoilt little boy, Olvir, started off by whining and complaining that he didn't like whatever Groa gave him to eat. But when he was told that if he didn't eat it, he would go hungry, he soon stopped fussing. Bard thought that his half-brother might grow up to be quite nice after all if he lived with Groa long enough.

There had not been any rain for many weeks. The marshes were drying up, and it was easy to cut rushes for thatching without getting wet feet. It was so hot that Toki and Bard stopped running round and were quite content to sit and watch Thorfast, the old comb-maker at work. He did a good trade selling combs. Everyone in Jorvik had lice and nits in their hair, as their houses and bedding were dirty. They needed combs to clean their heads.

One day a man from the countryside brought Thorfast a load of red deer antlers that he had collected. Thorfast paid the man in silver. The boys helped Thorfast to carry the antlers into his workshop. He was very grateful and said that he would teach them to carve runes, the characters that he used for writing people's names on the combs they bought.

He scratched all the letters in a line on a piece of wood, saying the name of each one. Then he showed the boys the letters that made their names. He looked through his stock of combs and picked out a comb for each boy. Then he set them to cut their own names on their combs.

Toki and Bard often stopped to talk to Snarri the jeweller. He never minded the boys coming into his dark workshop. He made all sorts of brooches for men and women. Men wore a big brooch on one shoulder to fasten their cloaks. Women whose husbands were rich bought a pair of brooches to wear one on each shoulder. They fixed strings of pretty glass and amber beads between the brooches, across the front of their dresses. Everyone could tell from a woman's ornaments how rich her husband was, so men liked to buy expensive brooches from Snarri for their wives. Rich men could buy brooches of gold and silver, but Snarri also made brooches of other metals that looked almost like gold and silver if you did not look too closely.

There were no banks in Viking towns where people could keep their gold and silver safe so rich Vikings *wore* their wealth in the form of brooches and other ornaments. Craftsmen made these by melting down the metal in a small clay pot called a crucible and then pouring the molten metal into moulds. This page shows how jewellery was made in Jorvik.

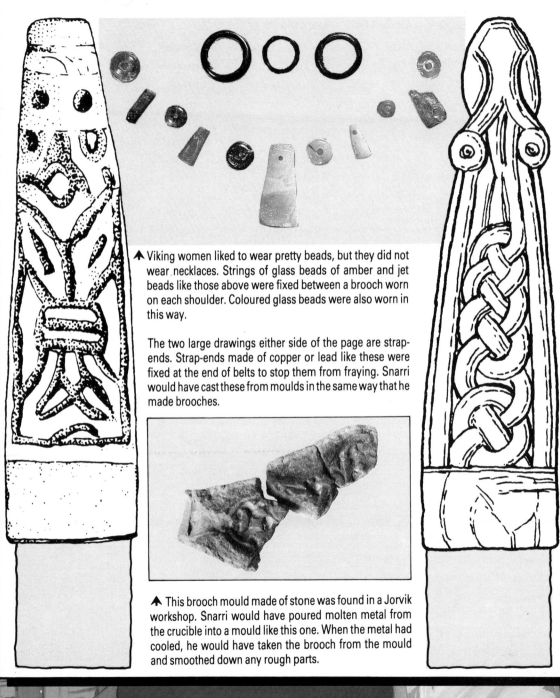

▲ Viking women liked to wear pretty beads, but they did not wear necklaces. Strings of glass beads of amber and jet beads like those above were fixed between a brooch worn on each shoulder. Coloured glass beads were also worn in this way.

The two large drawings either side of the page are strap-ends. Strap-ends made of copper or lead like these were fixed at the end of belts to stop them from fraying. Snarri would have cast these from moulds in the same way that he made brooches.

▲ This brooch mould made of stone was found in a Jorvik workshop. Snarri would have poured molten metal from the crucible into a mould like this one. When the metal had cooled, he would have taken the brooch from the mould and smoothed down any rough parts.

The boys liked to see Snarri pouring molten metal from a crucible into his moulds. It was like magic to see the metal cool into shiny brooches with patterns all over them. Snarri's jolly wife Thora had cheeks as red as apples. If she knew the boys were in the workshop, she would come in with some hot bread she had just baked, and cheese or honey to eat with it, saying that they must be hungry.

Snarri melted the metal to cast his brooches on a glowing charcoal fire on the big hearth in his dark little workshop.

One day a herd of cattle was being driven down the street when one of them broke away. It was chased by the herd dog, and blundered right into Snarri's workshop while Snarri was outside showing his wares to a customer. There was a dreadful clattering and sounds of things being knocked over. As the terrified bullock was being chased it plunged across Snarri's hearth scattering glowing embers all over the floor. In no time at all, storage baskets, the work table, and beeswax kept for casting were on fire. When Snarri smelled the burning wax, he gave a great shout and rushed into the burning workshop to save his precious stocks of old silver and gold things for melting down.

The fire took hold quickly, and flames shot up through the roof thatch.

The heat from the flames was terrible. No-one could get into the workshop to get Snarri out.

Everyone who lived nearby rushed to their homes to rescue their most precious possessions. They knew that the fire would spread from one house to another, as the houses were so close together. Some people fetched buckets of water from the wells and tried to put out the fire. Toki and Bard staggered along with a heavy wooden bucket each. But the flames spread so quickly that a line of four houses were soon burning fiercely. Women stood outside crying, as they saw their food stocks and everyday things burn up. It was terrible to see the cloth that had taken them so long to weave on their looms smouldering and crumbling into ash.

There were no matches in Viking times. A cooking fire had to be lit by striking a piece of iron against a flint. This made a hot spark fall on the tinder (a little heap of dry grass and leaves), which would burst into flames. Once a fire was alight the lady of the house would be very careful not to let it go out or spread beyond the hearth. Viking children must have spent many hours collecting fire wood.

◄ This wooden bucket was found in Norway. It is made of yew-wood and is bound together with strong metal hoops. Only fragments of buckets were excavated in Jorvik. Bard and Toki would have used a bucket like this to draw water from a well and to help put out the fire.

▼ This photograph shows that houses really did catch fire in Jorvik. It shows the burnt floorboards and wall posts of the corner of a house.

◄ Fire could easily spread from house to house in Jorvik because, as the photograph shows, the houses were built very close together. In the middle of each house was a big open hearth. This must have been a fire-risk in spite of having bricks set on edge all round to keep the hot embers together. Snarri, the jeweller, would have kept a fire burning all day in his workshop for melting down metal to make into jewellery.

Luckily the houses on the other side of the street were safe, as there was no wind to blow the flames across to their roofs.

Everyone was so busy watching the fire and wondering how far it would spread that they did not notice that the sky had clouded over. Suddenly there was a great clap of thunder and a patter of big raindrops. Sheets of rain swept down the street in a sudden gust of wind. The burning timbers hissed and the flames died down into smoke. There was a horrible smell of burning over the town. The rain had come just in time to stop the fire spreading right along the street, but that was no comfort to the families who had lost their houses and most of their goods.

Snarri's wife Thora had gone into the country that day to visit her daughter, who had married a farmer. When she came back, Toki's parents had to break the news to her that Snarri had died in the fire. She was very sad, as he had been a kind husband, and they had been married a long time. As her house was burnt with the workshop, she came to live with Toki's family, so there was still another person crowding round the hearth to eat the evening meal. But nobody minded. Thora was a plump, jolly person, and she helped Groa with the cooking and weaving. The children liked her very much.

On the evening of the fire, Toki and Bard were poking around among the nettles in their yard to look for eggs the hens had laid in places where they hoped they would be hard to find. Instead, they found Thora's poor cat, which had escaped from the burning house, but had all its fur burnt off. They put it in Toki's cloak and brought it into the house. Toki's father said that the best thing to do would be to put it out of its misery, but the children cried out, so Groa laid the cat in a nest of soft cloth. The children gave it milk. The poor bald thing hardly looked like a cat at all. But it gradually got better, and its fur and claws grew again. Surprisingly it gave birth to two kittens. Toki kept one, and gave the other to Bard's sister Drifa.

When people had collected all they could find from the remains of their homes, they asked Toki's father Gest to build new ones. So there was plenty of work for Gest that autumn.

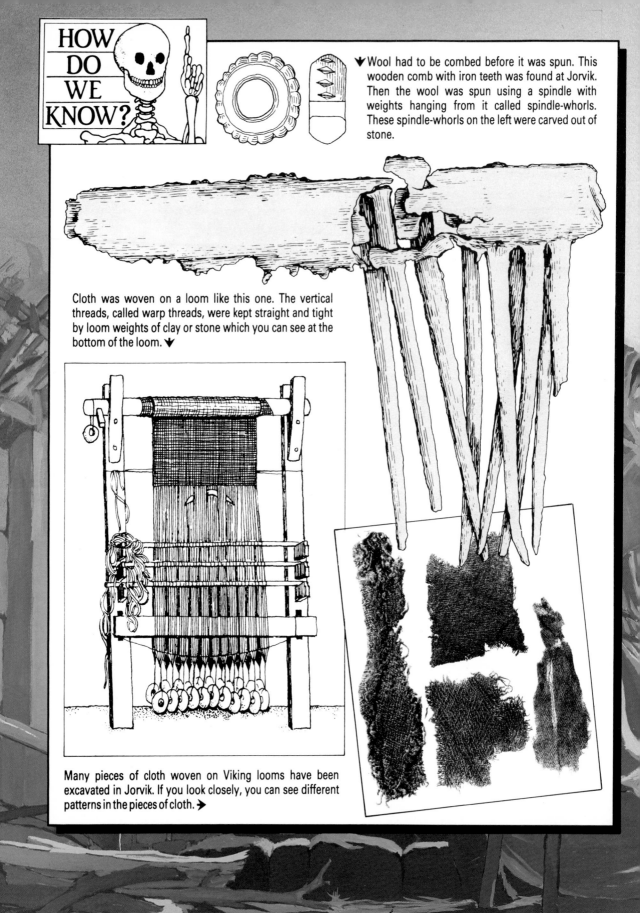

Wool had to be combed before it was spun. This wooden comb with iron teeth was found at Jorvik. Then the wool was spun using a spindle with weights hanging from it called spindle-whorls. These spindle-whorls on the left were carved out of stone.

Cloth was woven on a loom like this one. The vertical threads, called warp threads, were kept straight and tight by loom weights of clay or stone which you can see at the bottom of the loom. ✦

Many pieces of cloth woven on Viking looms have been excavated in Jorvik. If you look closely, you can see different patterns in the pieces of cloth. ➤

*Adventure on the Ice*

Life was different in winter. There were no foreign ships with exciting cargoes to watch on the waterfront. Seamen always returned to their homes in late summer, so as to avoid the gales and storms of autumn and winter.

In winter men made handles for tools, or mended carts and wagons in the shelter of farm buildings. It was a time when everyone found jobs to do indoors. Women sat at their looms, or spun the wool to be dyed in bright colours.

It was dark early, and people gathered round the hearth, where the fire gave some light in spite of the smoke drifting up to filter out through the thatched roof. The flames leapt up reflecting in the blades of tools hung on the wooden walls of the house. Rushlights flickered on spikes stuck into the timbers. The house was cosy as the floor was dug below ground level, but gusts of cold air swirled in when anyone came in from outside.

All the year round, the children of Jorvik had to look for firewood. All wood was precious, as so much was burnt on cooking fires and in furnaces for smelting metal and in pottery kilns. Men from the country brought loads of firewood into Jorvik to sell. Every house had a pile of logs against the wall ready for the winter.

There had been a lot of rain in the early part of the winter. After the storm that had luckily put out the fire, it seemed as if it would never stop raining. Toki and Bard were wet all the time. Everyone's clothes steamed when they came in and sat by the fire.

Bard was still Toki's best friend.

One morning Toki went into the yard early to go to the cesspit. The weather had changed. The sky was blue, and the

Vikings liked to decorate the things they bought or made with patterns. You can see from one of the pictures on this page that the Vikings liked a pattern made of a band twisted in or out, or plaited. These twisted patterns are called *interlace*, a word that means 'laced between'. Sometimes animals, like dragons, were woven into these interlaced patterns.

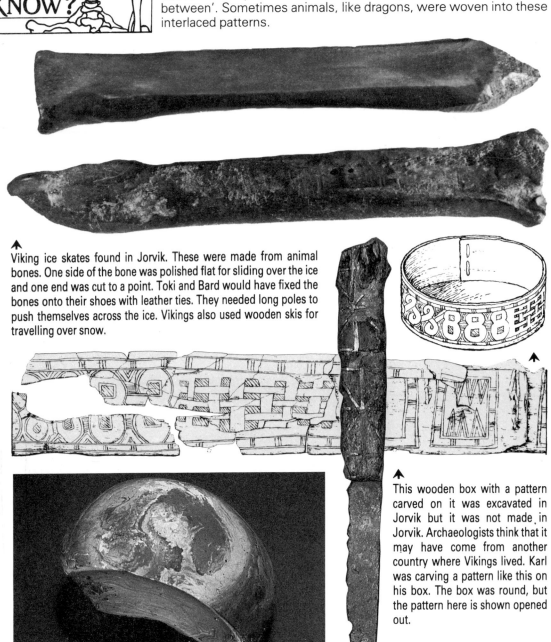

↑ Viking ice skates found in Jorvik. These were made from animal bones. One side of the bone was polished flat for sliding over the ice and one end was cut to a point. Toki and Bard would have fixed the bones onto their shoes with leather ties. They needed long poles to push themselves across the ice. Vikings also used wooden skis for travelling over snow.

↑ This wooden box with a pattern carved on it was excavated in Jorvik but it was not made in Jorvik. Archaeologists think that it may have come from another country where Vikings lived. Karl was carving a pattern like this on his box. The box was round, but the pattern here is shown opened out.

← Karl might have used a knife very much like this one for carving the pattern on his wooden box.

↑ A Viking smoother or iron made of glass found in Jorvik.

sun was shining, although there was not much heat in its pale rays. The grass and dead stalks of nettles growing in the yard were white with frost. Ice on the puddles crunched under his feet. The weather stayed cold and crisp for several days. The mud in the yard and street was hard and icy. The children came in early and got in Groa's way as she was cooking or weaving.

One morning she sent them all off into the country outside Jorvik to find firewood.

'Take your skates,' she said, although she thought that the boys would probably spend so long skating that they would not come back with much wood. Drifa wanted to go with the boys, and in the end they agreed. Bard made a fuss when Groa said they must take his little brother Olvir with them, but he had to come too.

It took a long time to find the bone skates, as they had been put away in a loft at the end of the last winter. They found some that were small enough for Drifa and Olvir that Toki had worn when he was little. Toki was relieved to find the skates. He thought that someone might have thought they were just old bones and had thrown them away with the rubbish. The boys tested the leather straps to see that they were still strong enough to bind the skates on over their shoes.

Groa saw the children off, telling them to be sure to be back before dark. She heaved a sigh of relief as she shut the door behind them and looked forward to a quiet day with Thora.

Thora sat on a stool by the fire working. She was making braid for the border of a new dress. Groa took out a big board and a glass smoother. As all the children were out, she could spread out a big piece of cloth and smooth the creases out of it. The cloth was a lovely orangy-red. She had dyed the wool herself, using madder roots. She was going to cut out a dress. After she had smoothed the cloth, she cut out the pieces with shears and began to sew them together with an iron needle and some linen thread. The two women talked happily.

Groa's father Karl had been out early to see his friend Eymundr, but he came home about the middle of the day. He lit some rush lights, as it was dark indoors. He took out a knife and sat carving a small round wooden box.

After a time, Groa expected the children home, so she put her work away and began to prepare the evening meal. She blew up the embers of the fire and put on some more wood. Thora fetched a bucket of water from the well. She came back saying that it was getting dark, and was colder than ever.

Archaeologists find pieces of broken pots wherever Vikings lived, as pottery does not decay. Archaeologists can find out what the pots were used for by sticking the pieces together and by looking at their different shapes. By studying the clay, scientists can date them and tell where they were made. In Jorvik we know that some pots came from the Rhineland, but many were made locally.

↓ This Viking horse shoe was excavated in Jorvik. The pot shown below was made in Jorvik from local clay. Groa would have used a pot like this one for cooking.

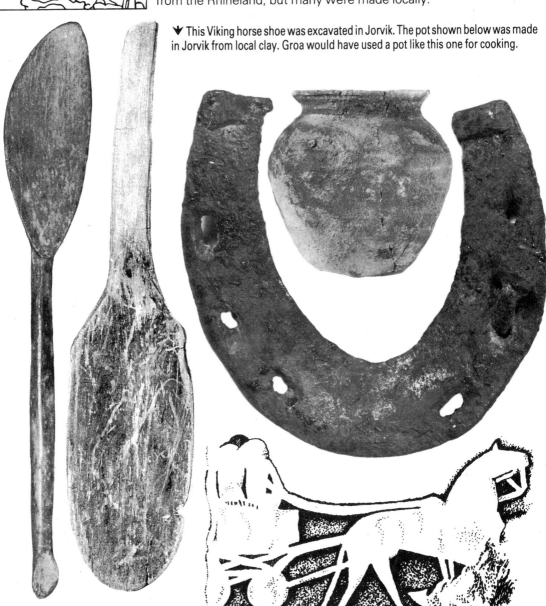

↑ These wooden spoons were found in Jorvik. While she was cooking, Groa would have stirred the pot with a wooden spoon like one of these.

↑ The wagon above was carved on a gravestone which was discovered in Sweden. The countryman's wagon on which he brought the children back home could have looked very much like the one in the drawing above.

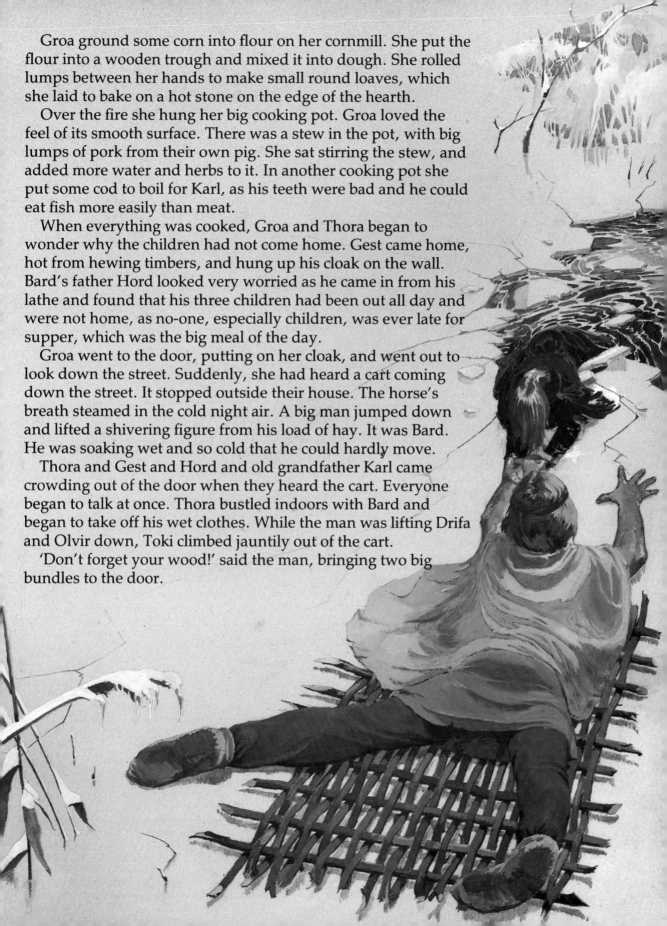

Groa ground some corn into flour on her cornmill. She put the flour into a wooden trough and mixed it into dough. She rolled lumps between her hands to make small round loaves, which she laid to bake on a hot stone on the edge of the hearth.

Over the fire she hung her big cooking pot. Groa loved the feel of its smooth surface. There was a stew in the pot, with big lumps of pork from their own pig. She sat stirring the stew, and added more water and herbs to it. In another cooking pot she put some cod to boil for Karl, as his teeth were bad and he could eat fish more easily than meat.

When everything was cooked, Groa and Thora began to wonder why the children had not come home. Gest came home, hot from hewing timbers, and hung up his cloak on the wall. Bard's father Hord looked very worried as he came in from his lathe and found that his three children had been out all day and were not home, as no-one, especially children, was ever late for supper, which was the big meal of the day.

Groa went to the door, putting on her cloak, and went out to look down the street. Suddenly, she had heard a cart coming down the street. It stopped outside their house. The horse's breath steamed in the cold night air. A big man jumped down and lifted a shivering figure from his load of hay. It was Bard. He was soaking wet and so cold that he could hardly move.

Thora and Gest and Hord and old grandfather Karl came crowding out of the door when they heard the cart. Everyone began to talk at once. Thora bustled indoors with Bard and began to take off his wet clothes. While the man was lifting Drifa and Olvir down, Toki climbed jauntily out of the cart.

'Don't forget your wood!' said the man, bringing two big bundles to the door.

This iron-bound wooden chest, with a padlock, was found in Norway, but parts of a chest very similar to this one were excavated in Jorvik. Groa kept all of her best possessions in a chest like this one. It might have been her grandfather's sea-chest if he had gone raiding. Vikings sat on chests like this one to row, keeping their share of the loot safely locked up inside.

The cream-coloured jar with red decoration you can see below was restored from pieces found in Jorvik. Many pieces of jars similar to this one were found showing that a great amount of wine was shipped from the Rhineland to Jorvik. Hord went home to fetch a jar of this wine to celebrate the children's safe return home and to thank the countryman. ⬇

⬆ The hurdle in the photograph above was excavated in Jorvik. It was laid on the ground to make part of a path. The countryman used a hurdle like this to rescue Bard.

Groa would have lit a lamp like this for extra light. The lamp, made of stone or clay, fitted over a long iron stake and was fixed in the ground wherever it was needed. The wick floated in melted fat in the bowl of the lamp. ⬇

What a tale they had to tell! Toki begged that their new friend should come in and eat with them, as he had saved Bard's life. Groa invited him to come in. The man agreed, but said that first he must tell his Jorvik friends that he had arrived with their load of hay, and stable his horse.

Soon they were all eating round the fire. The countryman was very shy, and he hardly managed to get a word in to answer everyone's questions. Toki said that they had been skating all day, pushing themselves along on the ice with poles so that they slid a long way. They remembered to gather some sticks from a wood, but came home a different way over the ice-covered marshes. They must have come to a patch of thin ice over deep water, because there had been a creaking and cracking sound, and Bard had suddenly disappeared through the ice. Toki lay down and managed to grab Bard's hair. Drifa and Olvir had cried, but Toki made them stop wailing and shout for help as loudly as they could.

The countryman said that he had heard them and had guessed what had happened. He had taken a hurdle from his cart so that he could lie on it and get near enough to the hole in the ice to drag Bard out.

The children had been very lucky, as he was passing by much later than he had meant to, and there was nobody else about at that time of day. They had all snuggled down into the load of hay for the ride into Jorvik.

Hord was so grateful to the countryman that he insisted on going home to fetch a lovely cream-coloured jar of Rhenish wine. Groa lit extra lamps as it was a special celebration. She unlocked the chest where they kept their best things, and got out their drinking horns with silver rims. It was a merry evening, and everyone was very thankful that the children were none the worse for their adventure on the ice.

# *Later that winter. . . . .*

There was more excitement later that winter.

Every night after supper Thora and Hord used to sit playing a game called hnefatafl. Sometimes people who played this got very angry, and the one who was losing would tip up the board so the pieces went all over the floor. But Thora and Hord never quarrelled. One evening Hord asked Thora if she would marry him. All the children thought that this was a very good idea.

Thora liked cooking and weaving, and made Hord a good wife. She treated all the children equally, and did not spoil Olvir as his mother had done. Hord was much more cheerful, and even made spinning tops for his children – Toki got one too. Toki and Bard decided that it had been a good year.

---

**Where you can see the things in this book and other things like them:**

| | |
|---|---|
| **York** | Jorvik Viking Centre, Coppergate |
| | Castle Museum |
| | Yorkshire Museum |
| **London** | British Museum |
| **Edinburgh** | National Museum of Antiquities of Scotland |
| **Dublin** | National Museum of Ireland |
| **Norway** | University Museum of National Antiquities, Oslo |
| **Sweden** | State Historical Museum, Stockholm |
| **Denmark** | National Museum, Copenhagen |

See what you can find in your local museum.